POEMS
ON LOVE,
LIFE &
HOMELAND

Ara John
Movsesian

The Electric Press®
Irvine, California

POEMS ON LOVE, LIFE & HOMELAND

Ara John Movsesian

Library of Congress Control Number: 2022931532

ISBN 978-0-916919-06-1 (Softcover) Trade Paperback

ISBN 978-0-916919-07-8 (Hardcover)

Cover Design by Rob Williams

The Electric Press®
Irvine, California

Forward

This collection of poems comes from several of my various books and endeavors. For example, some poems come from my book *Pearls of Love: How to Write Love Letters and Love Poems* published in the early 1980's, while others come from my book *Love Poems for Cards & Letters* or *Armenia: A Journey Through History* written by Arra S. Avakian Sc.D, for which I wrote the poetry.

A number of my poems have never been published, especially those concerning youth and animals. A few are from my website LoveAndRomance360.com.

I present these to you in this book because many of you may never read my other books, thus, this will be your introduction to my works.

I believe poetry should be accessible so that when read, a poem evokes immediate emotion without the need for deep analysis.

I hope you enjoy the experience.

Ara John Movsesian

Dedicated With Love To

My Wife, Arax
&
Son, Artin

Table of Contents

Page	Name of Poem	Copyright Date	Originally Published
On Love, Life And Living			
3	Cycles	1983	Pearls of Love
4	My Broken Heart	1983	Pearls of Love
5	In Search of Love	1988	Love Poems FC&L
6	On Summer Nights	2001	LoveAndRomance360.com
7	One Way Love	1983	Pearls of Love
9	Eternity	2000	LoveAndRomance360.com
10	A Lover's Gift	1988	Love Poems FC&L
11	Another Time	2000	LoveAndRomance360.com
12	Science and Love	2011	LoveAndRomance360.com
14	Faith	2011	LoveAndRomance360.com
15	The Picture	1983	Pearls of Love
16	Fortunate	2001	LoveAndRomance360.com
17	The Recipe of Love	1988	Love Poems FC&L
18	Excitement	2011	LoveAndRomance360.com
19	Valentine's Day	2022	Poems on Love L&H
20	Needs	1983	Pearls of Love
21	Take a Chance	1991	LoveAndRomance360.com
23	The Secret Garden	2001	LoveAndRomance360.com
25	Two Birds	1983	Pearls of Love
26	Unselfish Love	2022	Poems on Love L&H
27	Elegance	2022	Poems on Love L&H
28	Friendship and Love	2022	Poems on Love L&H
30	The Beauty of Your Book	2022	Poems on Love L&H
32	Devotion	2022	Poems on Love L&H
34	A Wish for My Friend	1988	Love Poems FCL
35	Jasmine, Rose and Daisy	1983	Pearls of Love
36	On Gossamer Wings	1983	Pearls of Love
37	Well-Tempered Love	1983	Pearls of Love
39	A Plain Old Kiss	1983	Pearls of Love
40	Harbor of Love	2011	LoveAndRomance360.com

Page	Name of Poem	Copyright Date	Originally Published
41	Pearls	1988	Love Poems FC&L
42	Kissing You Again	2001	LoveAndRomance360.com
43	In Your Lovely Eyes	1988	Love Poems FC&L
44	The Wanderer	1984-2022	Poems on Love L&H
46	To My Friend	1984-2022	Poems on Love L&H
47	Life	1984-2022	Poems on Love L&H
49	Spring	1979 -2022	Poems on Love L&H
51	The Living Force	1979-2022	Poems on Love L&H

On Children, Childhood And Animals

Page	Name of Poem	Copyright Date	Originally Published
55	The Animals Are Restless	1990-2022	Poems on Love L&H
56	Rocks	1990-2022	Poems on Love L&H
57	River Horse	1990-2022	Poems on Love L&H
58	Dirt	1990-2022	Poems on Love L&H
59	Pleasant Dreams	1990-2022	Poems on Love L&H
60	Kangaroo	1987-2022	Poems on Love L&H
62	Johnny and Ronny	1990-2022	Poems on Love L&H
65	A Fish! A Fish!	1990-2022	Poems on Love L&H

On My Homeland And People

Page	Name of Poem	Copyright Date	Originally Published
69	The Armenians	1998	Armenia: AJTH
72	Ararat	1998	Armenia: AJTH
73	Avarayr	1984-1998	Armenia: AJTH
75	David of Sasoun	1998	Armenia: AJTH
79	Etchmiadzin	1998	Armenia: AJTH
81	Aghtamar	1998	Armenia: AJTH
83	Ani	1998	Armenia: AJTH
85	Komitas	1998	Armenia: AJTH
88	Andranik	1998	Armenia: AJTH
90	An Old Man	1979-1998	Armenia: AJTH

On
Love, Life
&
Living

Wildflowers – A Watercolor by Marjorie Rodgers
First Published in Love Poems for Cards & Letters

છ૭

Cycles

Wildflowers bloom on a mountainside,
As icy waters on their tumbling ride,
Flow in haste to meet the Sea,
On a cycle that will always be.

Cycles, cycles everyplace,
Even in my life, I face,
The fact that cycles often race
With no regard to proper pace.

So I was born and grew up fast,
And now I'm free to love at last,
And need you to complete the chain
Of the cycle that is in my name.

ΣΟ

My Broken Heart

You possess the fury of a spring storm,
  The gentleness of a tropical shower.
You have a charm which is quick to warm
  The coldest men's hearts and make love flower.
Michelangelo must have sculpted you;
  Truly perfect is your figure and face;
Your soft, silken hair with its golden hue;
  An image to adorn a Roman vase.
You do not know how much I crave your kiss,
  For spirit free and innocent are thee.
You cannot know the pain of love's abyss,
  Nor can you see my eyes' impassioned plea.
With great charm and beauty, you lure my heart;
  Then, with abandon, you break it apart.

Sailing Boats - A Watercolor by Marjorie Rodgers
First Published in Love Poems for Cards & Letters

In Search of Love

Onto the Sea, I sailed my boat,
   And prayed that it would stay afloat;
From dawn till dusk - from dusk till dawn,
   In search of love, I drifted on;
What happened then, I don't recall -
   I think it was a sudden squall;
For when I awoke, I thought I'd died,
   At the sight of an Angel at my side;
But lucky for me, that was not true,
   For I'd found Love, and Love was you.

&

On Summer Nights

The twenty-first of June, my love,
 Is here and then, it's gone.
The days are long - the nights divine
 Until each break of dawn.

I long for Summer's entry;
 The pace of life - the sights;
But most of all, I long each day
 For your love on Summer nights.

I can't express in proper terms,
 The joys, the pleasures and delights,
That are a gift from you, my sweet,
 And your love on Summer nights.

True fortune has befriended me,
 It lifts me to wondrous heights,
From where my life is truly blessed,
 By your love on Summer nights.

೮೧

One Way Love

A one way love can never thrive;
  It needs reciprocation.
And so in order to survive
  My love needs affirmation.

So throw your caution to the sky,
  And let your heart command.
You'll find that it will not deny
  A love which must expand.

Come now, to me, with open arms
  And sweep me off my feet;
And then display for me your charms,
  To make my love complete.

My one way love will terminate
  Without your inspiration.
So, therefore, please reciprocate
  With no more hesitation.

છ

True love is a precious occurrence. All of us are searching for it and some of us find it and bask in its light. The poem Eternity celebrates such a love.

∽

Eternity

I smile whenever I recall
  The special moments we have had;
Walking always hand in hand
  Through the good times and the bad.

Sometimes, I think it is a dream --
  The love you give me could not be;
But then when you are in my arms
  There's no mistake in its purity.

Whether I'm with you or far away,
  My thoughts are always drawn to you
Like a compass needle pointing North
  To a love much more than true.

Of all the people on this Earth --
  How lucky can a person be;
To have found the likes of you, my love,
  With whom to share eternity!

∽

A Lover's Gift

Sometimes words can be obstacles,
As real as any mountain chain,
Or raging river running swift;
Sometimes words can cause great pain
And create a lover's rift.

But words can also fix bridges
And heal wounds;
Words can spirits lift;
And so, with this verse, I send
My sincerest lover's gift –

To cause the pain you feel to end;
To right the wrong of words untrue;
From my heart – three words to mend;
And they are simply – I love you!

∽

Another Time

The fragrance of an orchid
Wafting through the air,
Reminds me of another time,
And of a beauty rare.

The melodic strains of an orchestra
Sailing through the night,
Remind me of another time,
And of a lovely sight.

Associations such as these
Fill my thoughts with rhyme
And I can't help but long for
The poetry of another time.

A time when life made sense to me,
When love was everywhere;
When you and I would dance and dance
While your fragrance filled the air.

Such memories consume me,
And they constantly remind;
That you, my sweet, are in my heart
And forever on my mind.

&

Science and Love

A drop of water from the brook,
  Is void of life when first I look;
Revealing naught with the naked eye,
  Until through science, I apply
A microscope to make things clear
  And realize a new frontier,
Filled with life abundantly –
  A place of wonder and agony.

And so, the world in which I live
  To the drop of water is relative;
From space afar, I will not see
  with the naked eye, the panoply,
Until through science, I apply
  A telescope to clarify
That there exists upon this sphere
  As in the drop, a vast frontier.

(continues on the next page)

The multitudes that populate,
  To each other, love and hate;
This, I see with the naked eye,
  And don't need science to magnify
The fact that life is insecure;
  For this, I know there is no cure;
And always forces good or bad,
  Will bring us joy or make us sad.

But through it all, there is a light,
  That always shines upon me bright;
This, I see with the naked eye,
  And don't need science to verify,
That you, my sweet, are the steady source
  Of my good fortune – of this great force,
That strengthens me and nurtures my soul –
  That gives me love and makes me whole.

&

Faith

What does the word "faith"
   Mean to you?
      I don't think you really know,
         Why? Because your actions tell me so.
For example, you are always
   Jealous if anyone looks at me.
You should be pleased they do –
   At least, I'm not homely.
Have confidence in yourself
   And the good you have within you;
The good that I see everyday --
   That keeps me with you constantly.
If you don't have faith,
   You will always be miserable;
     And that can only lead
      To heartache.
Faith in my love for you
   Will set you free of doubt
     And give you peace of mind
   Permitting our love for each other
     To grow greater and fulfill its promise.

৪০

The Picture

Your picture which I have in hand,
  By itself could never stand;
For in dimensions, it does lack
  The third and foremost of the pack.

It will not kiss me on command;
  It cannot love me on demand;
And warmth, it never can imbue
  To this poor soul who yearns for you.

Torture me no more, my sweet;
  Pictures can't such passions treat;
And if they burn as mine do now,
  They need to be relieved somehow.

Thus, to this truth, I do adhere,
  That only you, my Doctor dear,
In three dimensions, can you clear
  This burning which is so severe.

So fly to me - do not delay;
  I cannot wait another day;
And free me from the torments of
  This raging three-dimensioned love.

80

15

Fortunate

I think you are sensational,
 Spectacular and more;
Your luscious lips and charming smile
 Are things, I can't ignore.

The sound of your alluring voice -
 The way you call my name;
You can't begin to understand
 How you set my heart aflame.

And whenever you are in my arms;
 Your body soft, sublime...
Gives me a taste of Heaven
 And stills the march of time.

You are an inspiration;
 You're entrancing and divine;
So fortunate am I, my love
 To know that you are mine.

ഇ

16

The Recipe of Love

The recipe of love must always include
Some herbs and spices for fortitude;
A tablespoon of forgiveness -
A clove of loyalty -
A cup of faith -
And a sprig of honesty;
A pinch of patience -
A teaspoon of trust -
A cup of friendship -
And a bit of lust;
Mix all these herbs and spices well -
No other recipe could ever excel;
Add a woman and man for proper effect;
Then sauté the whole in two cups of respect.

❧

17

Excitement

When I think of you,

I feel excitement come over me;

A rush of adrenalin

Through my veins

Revving up my heart –

Dilating my pupils –

Causing anticipation

At the thought of our

Next encounter;

Sometimes, I can't think

Of anything else

Except you – in my arms –

Savoring your sweet kiss

And the warmth of

Your loving embrace.

ॐ

Valentine's Day

Valentine's Day helps me convey --

Allows me to express what I seldom say;

Lets me open up and tell you how

Essential you are to me each day

Nurturing me with your affection;

Treating me to love's perfection;

Igniting passions not known before;

Nourishing my spirit and making it soar;

Enabling me to go confidently;

Saving me from uncertainty.

Destiny has been kind to me,

And you are the reason;

You are the key!

Needs

You don't need fancy jewelry

To make me fall for you.

You don't need a lot of makeup,

To cause me to pursue.

You don't need clothes from Gucci

To make me like you more.

You do not need to put on airs

To make my passions soar.

All you need is honesty,

And a smiling face;

Sincerity and loyalty,

And a warm embrace.

ဆေ

Take A Chance

A chance encounter of the best kind -
   A meeting arranged by fate -
Two souls have come together
   Two hearts can now relate.

Exploring has uncovered
   A tender love sublime,
Whose roots are strong and deep,
   To withstand the test of time.

This much, I know within my heart,
   That you are meant for me;
To share with me the joys of life;
   Throughout eternity.

So now, I ask with an open heart
   Barring my soul to thee;
Will you, my sweet, my soulmate
   Take a chance and marry me?

છ

Gardens are lovely places that provide peace of mind and a calming
atmosphere. Filled with Nature's handiwork, they symbolize
God's plan on this earth. Enjoy them whenever you have the chance to
savor their delights.

The next poem "The Secret Garden" symbolizes a pure Love that
nurtures and binds two hearts together.

෮෨

The Secret Garden

There is a light that shows me the way,
  To a secret garden, with a fragrant bouquet,
And as I enter through its welcoming gates,
  To savor all that for me awaits -
I can't help but wonder why the light chose me
  Why fate gave me the Garden's key.

For whatever the reason, this much I know,
  It is a lovely place where I love to go -
A garden full of life's delights -
  Of tenderness and wondrous nights.
A garden in which to nourish my soul;
  A place to go to make me whole
Where the warming light beckons me stay
  Where always it is Valentine's Day.

Time has shown me this simple truth,
  That the light that shines from high above -
That leads me to this garden each day
  Is the nurturing light of your infinite love.

෯

Swallows mate for life. When one gets hurt, the other tends to its needs and nurtures it back to health. When one dies, the other grieves. It is the ultimate expression of Love in its purest form.

⊗

Two Birds

Two birds begin a journey long,
   From different points in a far off land;
With a luring urge - in heart a song,
   Two novices heed life's command.

As they make their great migration,
   Their feeble feet turn to taloned hands;
And the two reach their destination
   As seasoned travelers in the northern lands.

Still unaware that the other lives,
   Each alights upon the very same tree;
And there the two, as if guided by God,
   Fall madly in love and marry.

Thus so it is with you and me;
   Two birds which Heaven's winds did blow
To this blessed rendezvous of life,
   Like the two swallows at Capistrano.

෯

Unselfish Love

You say you love me very much;
   You show your affection with your touch;
But when I ask you to align
   With some wish or want of mine,
You find some reason to decline.

But on the other hand, when you
   Have something that you want to do,
I go along with no complaint;
   And if need be, myself acquaint
With what you do without restraint.

In light of this, I must conclude,
   That you have a selfish attitude,
That needs to be corrected fast –
   Or else our love will never last;
And very soon, it will have passed.

So with this knowledge, I implore
   That you, my sweet, somehow restore
My faith in "us" and your commitment to
   A meaningful change that will renew
An unselfish love between me and you.

≈

Elegance

You have an air about you;
An aura; a technique!
That sets you off from all the rest –
That makes you quite unique.

The way you walk through time and space –
The graceful moves you make;
The poetry of your motion
Is a pleasure to partake.

Your voice is the music of the spheres,
Melodic in every way;
A feast of grand sensations,
Worthy of the best gourmet.

The clarity of the way you think,
So simple, sincere and sound,
Combines logic, love and truth,
To make all thoughts profound.

Such qualities when all combined,
Are of great significance,
Because, summed up in a single word,
You are "elegance!"

ᔓ

Friendship and Love

What can I say to you
    That can properly express my appreciation
For your thoughtfulness and companionship?

As you know, I have many acquaintances
    And so-called friends,
But I confess that only you
    Define the term "friendship"
To its fullest extent.

You ask, what do you mean?
    Well, like new-fallen snow,
You blanket me with the purity of your heart –
    And you have no pretenses or agendas
Of any type!

(continues on the next page)

Like a symphony, you give me pleasure
    Every time I hear your silken voice
Whether in song
    Or in every day conversation.

In this selfish world,
    You are a delightful summer breeze
Bringing with it
    Your kind and caring ways.

And when you comfort me
    And help me find my way
Through the difficult times of my life,
    I feel blessed that you are present
To give me your wisdom and guidance.

What truly have I done to deserve you?
    How have I become so fortunate?
To be the receiver of your friendship
    Which, in my heart,
I know is the prerequisite of love?

಄

The Beauty of Your Book

"Belle," in French, is a lovely word
   Expressing a pleasant sight;
   And when I see you standing there,
   You give me great delight.

"Elegant" is a charming term,
   Describing the way you walk;
   Defining how you handle yourself,
   And the alluring way you talk.

(continues on the next page)

"Appealing" is an expressive word,

Describing how you move me
For only you attract me so,
That each night is poetry.

"Understanding" is the perfect term,

Expressing how you are;
How you help me find needed peace of mind
My compass — My bright North Star.

"Tender" is an ideal word

Describing your soft, sweet kiss;
Something, I can't get enough of,
Giving me Heavenly bliss.

"Youthful" is the optimum term

Defining the way you look;
Rounding out all of your attributes
Completing the beauty of your book.

&

Devotion

True love requires choice ingredients
   To balance the recipe;
To give the proper sweetness,
   And even some acidity.

The first is "loyalty,"
   To each other, all of the time;
It gives a relationship flavor'
   It gives it rhythm and rhyme.

The second is "Faith,"
   In the person one holds dear;
It is the glue that ties the two,
   And drives away all fear.

The third is "dedication,"
   To strengthen the bonds that bind;
On both sides of the equation,
   In body and in mind.

(continues on the next page)

The fourth is a "forgiving heart,"

Pure and without pretense,

Essential for Love's perfection,

And for its permanence.

The fifth and most important one

Is "devotion" to the nth degree -

Serving as the matrix in which love exists

Like the salt that fills the Sea.

ℭ

A Wish for My Friend

You have proven to me firsthand,

    That you will always stand

At my side, in times of good - in times of woe,

    In rain or sleet or sun or snow;

And so I send this special wish,

    To a friend for a friendship

I will always cherish;

    May your life be filled with excellent health -

Much success and a bit of wealth;

    And may you live by the light above,

And feel the joys that come from love.

ℂ

34

Jasmine, Rose and Daisy

You are the Jasmine of all my senses;
    Your stunning beauty drops my defenses,
And I am stripped of all pretenses,
    As I accept all consequences.

You are the wild Rose of my heart;
    I yearn for you when we're apart,
For then my passions on fire start,
    Desperately desiring your lover's art.

You are the Daisy of my being;
    You give my soul a love enduring,
Which makes each day a day worth living,
    And makes you ever more alluring.

ᏸᎧ

On Gossamer Wings

When first we touched, my heart flew high,
    On gossamer wings, through a cloudless sky.
People told me this love would die,
    They said it was built upon a lie.

They told me my feelings would surely fade;
    Passions would cease and foes would be made.
To this I said, "Why are you so blind?"
    "Can you not put the past behind?"

True love can change a river's course,
    Or pierce the strongest vault with ease.
True love can turn coal into gold,
    Or tame the Tempest to a balmy breeze.

Quite some time has passed since then;
    People no longer criticize;
For now they see that truth exists,
    Where once there might've been only lies.

Thus my feelings are the same today,
    As they were on that very first day;
For when we touch, my heart still flies,
    On gossamer wings through cloudless skies.

⟡

Well-Tempered Love

The fires of my loneliness,

     Once filled my life with much distress;

And constantly they did suppress

     My every chance at happiness.

In truth, I lost all zest for life,

     And every day was filled with strife;

Until, that is, the day you came

     Into my life and called my name.

With tenderness you gave to me,

     The strength to set my spirit free,

And then you showed me lovingly,

     How wonderful my life could be.

(continues on the next page)

As our new friendship grew and grew,
A joyous feeling did ensue.
I know that I was born anew,
When I realized my love for you.

This love has bounds I cannot see,
It is universal poetry;
And with its durability,
It shall continue endlessly.

So future trials will not repress;
Life's tribulations will not suppress
This well-tempered love which I possess;
Forged in the fires of my loneliness.

ॐ

A Plain Old Kiss

Some people need a peck or two;
   For others a simple smooch will do;
To many, a graze will stimulate;
   A few may want to osculate.

And then there are those who need a smack;
   For flowery words, they have a knack.
But all I want from you is bliss,
   Which you can give me with a plain old kiss.

෨෬

Harbor of Love

Everyone is set afloat
   Upon the open Sea of life
One day to languish in the doldrums,
   The next to battle the winds of strife.

Thus fortune, sometimes, upon me shines;
   And for a while, it is my fate;
But then it turns its solemn face -
   Uncertainty is life's sad state.

But you are a constant in my life,
   A welcome refuge from the turbulent Sea;
A haven for my battered soul -
   A safe harbor of love and certainty.

&

Pearls

There are many, many pearls in the sea;

Most are flawed to some degree;

But of all that are, and will ever be --

You are the most perfect pearl for me.

છ

Kissing Your Again

Sweet Spring is here, my dearest love;
The flowers are in bloom;
Their fragrance travels through the air
And floats into my room.

Grim Winter's grip upon our love.
Has given way, at last,
And now, we are able to share again
What we had in the past.

Pleasant memories flood my mind;
My heart begins to race,
At the thought of kissing you again
While in your warm embrace.

৪১

In Your Lovely Eyes

There is much beauty
  On this earth –
In stately trees
  And cloud-filled skies
But the greatest beauty
  I've ever seen
Is found
  In your lovely eyes

ဆၢ

The Wanderer

Home is but a memory lodged within my mind
Repressed in cracks and dulled by time
It cries for ages past
And you, no more, left miles and miles behind.

Long ago, my life's path changed,
Due to a storm wind that strongly blew;
My future plans were shattered
As was my life with you.

An urge with mighty influence
Swelling through my soul,
Caught me in a whirlpool,
And swept me through a hole.

I could not stay – I went away
To worlds beyond compare;
Searching for my rainbow's end
And for a dream so rare.

(continues on the next page)

Adventure, chills, excitement, thrills —
All of these, I've felt;
Yet never did I reach my goal
And in its glory knelt.

And as you gaze into your past,
    What will your thoughts display?
Triumphant voyages and exotic lands
    Or life so far away?

Or will you think of lowly me
    A wanderer alone?
And will you think of all we've missed
    Since I began to roam?

Yes, ages have, indeed, gone by
    And many things have changed;
For things I thought so normal then
    Have come to be so strange.

It puzzles me when I attempt
    To find an answer true;
The correlation being lost
    In the miles 'tween me and you.

જી

To My Friend

I woke up from a restful sleep,
    To meet a day of beauty;
But then I found out that a friend
    Had somehow died and left me.

Suddenly, the day grew cold;
    The sun departed – winds began to blow;
And in my grief, I left confused,
    To spend the day in deep sorrow.

Mere words cannot express enough,
    The emptiness I felt inside;
And the pain of a friendship now destroyed
    Was something from which, I could not hide.

Each thought that crossed my mind that day
    Was of my friend – the times we shared;
It was unfair, at least to me
    To lose a friend for whom I cared.

I guess that time will fill the void;
    Heal the wound and dull the pain;
And then my friend will live once more
    In precious memories which will remain.

☙

46

Galaxy NGC-4414

Life

Life –

    The mortal pathway,

        What there is 'tween near and far,

    All consciousness – unconsciousness,

        Existence in a jar.

Life –

    The road down which we go,

        Stumbling – Falling – Rising;

    What we do is what we are –

        Which isn't so surprising.

(continues on the next page)

Life –

Emptiness between two points
    Which must be filled with matter;
And through our actions, we determine
    How full will be the latter.

Life –

Non-existence for many
    Existence for a few;
To show that one has been and gone'
    Some worthy thing, one must do.

Life –

Depends on where we are,
    In a jar, a cage or free;
In the first, we can see – In the second, hear
    In the third, we can truly be.

Life –

Fulfillment or despair –
    The joy of helping one another -
The malevolence of selfishness –
    A gift from every mother.

ജ

Ice melting and replenishing the spring runoff

Spring

Snows Melt
Giving nourishment
To sleeping earth.

Skies unleash
Previously hidden
Components of living tissue.

Watercourses
Regain their stature
And transport goodwill.

(continues on the next page)

New life reaches up
From darkened depths
Grasping for the sun.

Denuded branches
Sprout new cover
Helping seed pods generate.

Inner time clocks
Begin renewing life,
While outlooks become optimistic.

What impulse lies
Behind this change?
And what has it to gain?

'Tis Spring!
Harold of new beginnings -
Giver of strength -
Whose presence is introduced
To jar all life from its stupor
And force it to begin anew!

&

The Living Force

As precious as a diamond
    Yet feared by all that lives
With a paradoxical nature
    It takes as well as gives.

As old a time itself
    And as new as morning dew
Sometimes a living Godsend
    At times a deathly coup.

With a texture so intriguing
    As changeable as dice
So hot or cold or in-between
    That can one name suffice?

Pervading all that live on earth
    Invading every sphere
A simple chain of atoms
    Which all life holds so dear.

Without it, we are helpless
    And with it, we are brave
But if too much is present
    Ourselves, we cannot save.

(continues on the next page)

It cannot be created
   Nor can it be destroyed
It is the basic staff of life
   That Nature has employed.

Whether it is welcomed
   Or whether it is scorned
WATER is the Living Force
   With which all life is formed.

ॐ

Iguazú Falls, Argentina & Brazil

On Children, Childhood & Animals

In the Forest - Watercolor by Marjorie Rodgers
From the children's book, Rinny Raccoon

&

The Animals Are Restless

A toad crosses the road,
    While a swan swims on and on;
And a bear goes down to its lair
    To spend the winter there.

A goose chases a moose,
    Honking angrily;
While a busy, busy bee
    Flies in circles around a tree.

An ant climbs slowly up a plant
    And a bat flies after a cat;
While a gopher digs a hole,
    And, by mistake, runs into a mole.

A mouse goes into a house,
    And a pig escapes from its pen;
While up above, there flies a dove,
    And a dog chases a quail, once again.

All the animals are restless –
    And so are the insects too!
Because they are all working together
    To make God's Plan come true.

℥

Rocks

Kerplunk! Kerplunk! The rocks fall down
 And splash into the calm, clear lake,
Disturbing fish that swim about,
 And causing reeds to shake.

Kerplunk! Kerplunk! The rocks come down
 And fall into the calm, clear lake,
Making all the ducks fly off,
 And all the sleeping frogs to wake.

Kerplunk! Kerplunk! The rocks fall down
 And splash into a great big mouth!
A mouth! Oh! No! A Crocodile!
 With rows of teeth and a hungry smile –
It's looking straight at me –
 With eyes that stare and see;
I think, I'd better run away,
 Cause he might eat me if I stay.

But, don't you worry, I'll be back!
 I really love the sound rocks make;
Kerplunk! Kerplunk! When they come down
 And splash into a calm, clear lake.

ॐ

River Horse

What swims in rivers like a fish -
    But weighs almost a ton?
What has a big mouth and grows four feet tall
    And hates the heat of the sun?

It lives all over Africa,
    And walks on four-toed feet;
And all it does is sleep and swim
    And eat and eat and eat!

In English, it's called a "River Horse;"
    But that means little to us;
Since we all know it by its Greek name –
    H-I-P-P-O-P-O-T-A-M-U-S !

ℂ

Dirt

Dirt is fun to play with
And on a hot day, it's cool;
I'd rather spend a day in dirt
Than spend a day in school!

With dirt, I make tall mountains,
Then I climb them just for fun;
Next, I dig the grandest canyons
Where raging rivers run.

Roads and valleys, hills and dales –
All these things, I make;
And then I drive my fastest car
Down the roads to my favorite lake.

"Enough of this," my mother shouts,
"It's time to go to school!"
Why does she act so cruel?
I'd rather spend a day in dirt,
Than spend a day in school.

૪૭

Pleasant Dreams

Gum drops, Ice cream, Jelly Beans –
   Chocolate Cookies – Pleasant Dreams;
In the morning, "Rise and Shine."
   "Wash your face and then feel fine."

"Eat your breakfast" – "Drink your juice,"
   "Don't fight with your sister" – "Call a truce!"
"Brush your teeth and comb your hair;"
   "Don't complain and please don't stare!"

"Off to school, by bus you go" –
   "Rain or shine or sleet or snow" –
"Learning things is such great fun"
   "And all your homework must be done!"

After dinner, play awhile,
   Then off to bed - without a smile?
Gum drops, Ice Cream, Jelly Beans –
   Chocolate Cookies – "PLEASANT DREAMS!"

છ૭

Kangaroo

Yesterday, my mom took me to the Zoo;
    And there, I saw a real Kangaroo;
She hippity-hopped,
    And then, she stopped –
She looked to the left –
    She looked to the right –
She looked straight at me,
    And then hopped out of sight!

(continues on the next page)

I waited and waited for her to come back,
  So while I stood there, mom bought me a snack;
All of a sudden, I heard the sound
  Of thumping feet upon the ground;
And there she was –
  But now there were two!
Mommy and baby Kangaroo.

This itty-bitty kangaroo
  Was the smallest baby at the Zoo –
It was so small, it could fit in my shoe;
  And it sat in a pocket on its mommy's tummy,
And it looked just like a puppet – just like a dummy;
  I could have stared and stared all day long,
But my mom took my hand and said, "Come along!"

I did not want to go away –
  I told my mom, "I want to stay!"
But she said "No!" "There is much to see,"
  "So hurry up now and come along with me."
As we walked away, I watched mommy kangaroo –
  With her cute little itty-bitty baby, too –
She looked to the left –
  She looked to the right –
She looked straight at me
  And then hopped out of sight.

୫ଠ

Johnny and Ronny

One day, Johnny saw little Ronny
  Running down the sidewalk;
"Wait a minute!" He shouted
  And ran over to talk.

"Have you seen big Donny?"
  He asked little Ronny;
"No, I haven't," Ronny said,
  "I think Donny's sick in bed."

(continues on the next page)

"Oh!" "That's bad!" said Johnny,
   "I was hoping he could play."
"It would be so much fun"
"Since there's no school today."

"I know what you mean,"
   Replied little Ronny;
But instead of big Donny,
   Let's ask our friend Lonny."

"That's a great idea," said Johnny,
   I really like our friend Lonny;"
"He is so much fun to play with;
   And throws the ball better than big Donny."

So Johnny and little Ronny
   Ran four blocks down the street
And finally reached Lonny's house
   With sore and aching feet.

When they rang the doorbell,
   Lonny's mom appeared
And then she told them
   what they both had feared.

"Why, Lonny is not here,"
   "He is with Bonny, today;"
"They went to his grandpa's farm"
   "To enjoy the animals, and play."

(continues on the next page)

Ronny wrinkled his nose –
   Johnny hung his head low;
Then they both turned around
   And started to go.

"Rats!" said Johnny
   "What a rotten trick!"
Our friend Lonny is with Bonny,"
   "And big Donny is sick!"

"What a boring day
   This is going to be;"
"There is nothing to do,"
   "And there is nothing to see."

"Yes there is, Johnny!"
   Said little Ronny;
"We can go see the movie"
   "My mom prepared for me."

"What a neat idea!"
   Johnny shouted with glee;
As they ran down the street,
   As happy as can be.

∛

A Fish! A Fish!

A fish! – A fish! – I see a fish!
   Swimming in the lake;
It's looking for food I think
   And making lilies shake.

I grab my fishing pole –
   My heart is beating fast;
I rush to bait my hook;
   And then I make my cast.

Plop! Into the water
   Goes my hook and bait;
I cross my toes – I hold my breath,
   And then I wait and wait.

(continues on the next page)

It seems like forever –
    And I almost pass out;
But then I feel a great big tug
    And another and another and I shout!

A fish! – A fish! – I have a fish!
    It's fighting hard to get away –
It's big – I think, it's big!
    I wonder how much it'll weigh.

All my friends will be jealous;
I know they will – they will!
Their eyes will pop open –
Their mouths will drop down
And I'll get such a thrill!

Then I'll take my big fish home,
So mom can cook it for me;
I can taste it now, Mmuh, Mmuh!
She'll use her best recipe.

Oh No! – Oh No! – It just fell off!
I see it swimming away!
I guess, I'll have to try again
To catch it some other day.

∛

On
My Homeland
&
People

The ruins of the Church of the Holy Redeemer – Built 1035 AD

Armenians are a melding of many peoples. You might say we are a hybrid of wanderers from many regions who settled in Anatolia (now known as Turkey).

Throughout our history, we have struggled to maintain our identity as hordes of conquerors have swept through our homeland intent on subjugating us. Because we adopted Christianity as a State religion in 451 AD, we still exist as a distinct ethnic group, where others have faded away.

෫ෟ

The Armenians

Sky plunges to earth; communes with stone;
    A jagged union so formed by God
That in its eerie polychrome,
    This land served as the seedling pod.

With hardened lines of massive rocks,
    Confronting gentle wisps of grass,
Whose tenacity to live and grow,
    Depends on roots to hold on fast.

And river valleys cleft in stone,
    Meander through this land of old;
While meadows full of Alpine life,
    Keep God's creatures in their fold.

Such a land of wide expanse -
    Of monoliths with weathered face
A battleground 'tween life and death
    Is home to a proud and noble race.

(continues on the next page)

First to grasp the Christian life,
    And fight to keep it their very own -
Great works attesting to their faith,
    They built to rise from sculpted stone.

For ages, hordes of conquerors
    Trampling o'er their ancient ground -
Killed, defaced, destroyed, disgraced -
    Yet never was their spirit bound.

Adversity did not deter
    This people from their will to be;
And nurtured by their faith in God,
    They hung on quite tenaciously.

Today, they still exist on Earth,
    While other peoples have come and gone
Armenians - with their hardy roots
    Are waiting for another dawn.

And as their mighty, symbol grand -
    Always watching from on high -
As if to lend a helping hand
    Rises Ararat to meet the sky!

Mt. Ararat with Khor Virap in the foreground
as seen from the eastern side in the Republic of Armenia

Mt. Ararat is the acknowledged resting place of Noah's Ark once the flood waters subsided, and for ages this noble mountain has symbolized the land of the Armenians, my people.

In 1994, I had the pleasure of visiting Mt. Ararat at its base in the western foothills of what was once called Anatolia (our ancestral lands).

ℰℭ

Ararat

As the light of day returns once more,
To the ancient land of Urartu;
Off in the distance, a mountain looms
Beckoning all for a rendezvous.

Rising up from surrounding soil,
Its peak always covered in white,
Ararat, the sentinel,
Stands aloof both day and night.

Since before recorded history,
Ararat has witnessed all;
The Flood and Noah and his Ark -
And watched countless martyrs fall.

As the light of day slowly fades away,
The symbol of Armenia stands;
As a beacon of hope for the future,
And guardian of all Armenian lands.

80

Vardan Mamigonian with Ghevond Yeretz Blessing the
Armenian Army on the Eve of the Battle of Avarayr

In 451 AD, Armenians fought the first ever battle for religious
freedom, and even though we lost that battle, we ultimately won
the war and never renounced our faith. As a result, Armenia became
the first nation in the world to adopt Christianity as its state
religion. Because of that, throughout the ensuing centuries, we
were able to keep our identity as Armenians.

Avarayr

The morning air so fresh and sweet -

The verdant valley full of life -

The flowing river clear and swift -

Quietly waiting for death and strife.

(continues on the next page)

Amassed on either side of glade;
  Tensed like Tigers stalking prey;
Two armies stood prepared to clash,
  To see whose strength would thus outweigh.

Yazdegerd and his mighty horde,
  Determined to confront and win;
To force upon Armenians all
  A god that was not genuine.

And Vardan and his army small;
  With Cross and Ghevond at his side;
Stood prepared to fight till death
  Against oppression from outside.

Thus, as the Sun's rays filled the sky,
  A thunderous roar disturbed the scene;
And suddenly, this peaceful place
  Became a hellish sight, obscene.

Avarayr, this valley faire,
  Was blessed with Vardan's blood that day,
And even though Armenians lost,
  Yazdegerd never got his way.

෪

74

Yervand Kochar's Statue of David of Sasoun – circa 1994
Yerevan, Republic of Armenia

There are many Armenian Folktales, but one of the most prominent is
the Legend of David of Sasoun in which David protects his people and
his land from the conqueror, Melik and his horde.

David of Sasoun

With Jelali, his trusty steed
His armor and his lightning sword,
David of Sasoun stands aloof
To slay the oncoming horde.

So fearless, so courageous -
So resolute is he,
That all who come to face him
To this, they all agree.

(continues on the next page)

As the son of Lion Meher,
Under Ohan's guiding hand,
David protects the livestock,
His people and his land.

Thus, one day as fate decrees
Melik and his horde arrive;
From Egypt, they descend
To conquer and deprive.

With Jelali, his trusty steed,
His armor and his lightning sword
David of Sasoun rides to Melik
To attack the oncoming horde.

The fighting is fast and very fierce;
He slays from left to right;
But Melik can't be found
On that horrendous night.

Then someone shouts, "Why fight us?
Your enemy lies there!
Within that tent asleep!
Go slay him, if you dare!"

David calls to Melik,
"Wake up and meet your fate."
And Melik calls to David,
"Come in, let us debate."

(continues on the next page)

As David enters Melik's tent,
He falls into a pit;
But the Patroness of Sasoun
Helps David to outwit.

Then Misra-Melik strikes a blow;
A vicious dual begins.
But in the end with his mighty sword
David of Sasoun wins.

With Jelali, his trusty steed,
His armor and his lightening sword
David of Sasoun triumphs
Over Melik and his horde.

Varaz Samuelian's Statue of David of Sasoun
Fresno, California – circa 1998

Etchmiadzin (The Descent of the Only Begotten Son) is the Mother See of the Armenian Apostolic Church erected in the 4th century AD by King Trdat III and St Gregory the Illuminator.

This cathedral is the seat of the Catholicos of All Armenians – the head of the national church. In 1996, I had the honor of singing in the Cathedral choir.

ℰℭ

Etchmiadzin

Son of God descending --
    With Golden Hammer in hand;
Striking ground - commanding
    A church be built to stand.

St. Gregory could not ignore
    A vision so profound,
And heeding Christ's command
    Built a Church on that Hallowed Ground.

Etchmiadzin, he called it -
    And he made it the Holy See;
Where the Catholicos of All Armenians
    And the "Mayr Ator" would be.

And as the beacon of our Christian Faith,
    Its light spread across the land;
Giving to all Armenians,
    A spiritual helping hand.

(continues on the next page)

From its simple and modest beginnings,
In the time of Trdat's reign;
The church was modified, embellished,
Destroyed and built again.

Beneath its arched and vaulted roof
The "Ijman Seghan" stands,
Showing all where His hammer struck
As He issued His commands.

Such stories could its walls recount
Of pagan and of darker days,
Of liturgies and sharakans ...
Of priests and deacons giving praise.

Today, there it stands as the symbol
Of Armenia's Christian past;
Proclaiming with its melodic bells,
The strength of a faith that will last.

&

("Mayr Ator" means "Mother Chair," in Armenian
"Ijman Seghan" is the name of "the table where it struck"
"Sharakans" means "Hymns in Armenian)

The Cathedral of the Holy Cross - Aghtamar Island, Turkey – circa 1994

The Catholicos of an independent See of the Armenian Apostolic Church was active there for eight centuries from 1113 to 1895 and the Cathedral of the Holy Cross on the island of Aghtamar was his church. I visited the cathedral in 1994 and chanted prayers on its altar.

Aghtamar

Lake Van's waters in hues of blue

Stretching out to infinity;

Surround the island called Aghtamar,

Giving it a pristine purity.

(continues on the next page)

Rising up from its rocky soil
 Is a work of art - a monument;
Created by man - inspired by God;
 A statement pure and eloquent.

Holy Cross - the Cathedral Church,
 Built by Gagik as the Holy See;
Adorned with carvings on its exterior
 Proclaiming a biblical history.

There, Jesus and Mary, Adam and Eve
 Are frozen in tufa for eternity;
Along with David, Goliath and Saints,
 As a form of sculptural poetry.

And faded frescoes on inside walls
 Attest to a great solemnity,
That took place beneath the circular dome
 Amid such balance and harmony.

Aghtamar is now a lonely place -
 And Holy Cross is an empty shell
The sweet strains of the Mass waft no more
 For Armenians there, no longer dwell.

&

82

The battlements (exterior walls) of the City of Ani located near Kars in eastern Turkey. Ani was the capital of the Bagratid Armenian kingdom from 961 AD to 1045 AD and is often referred to as the "City of 1001 churches." I visited this historic place and enjoyed walking around with the knowledge that my direct ancestors had lived there in its heyday - a thousand years before.

Ani

A great wall rises from the rocky soil,

    A battered boundary between dark and light;

The guardian of hallowed ground,

    The symbol of past power and might.

To pass beyond through its entrance arch,

    Crowned by a lion - devoid of gate;

Is to pass into the hazy past,

    Where lives and nations met their fate.

(continues on the next page)

Silence is now the rule of thumb,
    And barren is the landscape there;
Shorn of its many vestments grand,
    Through years of pillage, neglect and despair.

The wind blows gently through this emptiness,
    While wisps of grass seek the sun's rays;
Yet, from where they spring lie many buried stones,
    Forever still - now unused - ruins of greater days.

What memories do these stones contain
    Locked within and beneath the ground?
When will they see the light of day
    To let the voices within them sound?

The history that they will tell,
    Of Bagratids and churches grand;
Whose scattered ruins dot this somber soil,
    Whose altars now in silence stand.

Ani, the city of mighty kings,
    Once Armenia's sacred Holy See;
Is now but a shadow - frozen in time,
    Its grandness - only a memory.

ℰↃ

Komitas was born Soghomon Soghomonian in 1869 in Kutahya, Ottoman Empire (present day Turkey). He became an Armenian priest and is known as a musicologist, composer, arranger, singer, and choirmaster who is considered to be the founder of the Armenian national school of music. He collected the music of the Armenian homeland and composed, among many works, the Armenian Liturgy.

Komitas

Orphaned at a tender age,
    And sent to study at Etchmiadzin,
Soghomon with his pleasant voice
    Thrived in the musical discipline.

Once ordained a celibate priest,
    He traveled to study musicology;
Learning from the greats of that time
    Composition and forms of harmony.

(continues on the next page)

With formal studies at an end,
   He returned to the place where he began,
To teach to others what he had learned -
   To realize God's Holy Plan.

While there, his greatest works took shape:
   To collect the many songs of his land
And write them down to preserve them,
   As if moved by some divine command.

He then turned his thoughts to the Patarag;
   Arranging the Armenian Liturgy
As if guided by the hand of God
   He gave it a heavenly purity.

His life had many twists and turns,
   And on to Istanbul he went;
Where he showed the world what he had done,
   His arrangements - pure and eloquent.

On a dark and somber April night
   Komitas was led away,
To face a fate unthinkable
   That befell Armenians on that day.

(continues on the next page)

But, no, his fate was not the same
For Komitas was spared his life
By the intervention of Morganthau
He lived through all the pain and strife.

After the dirty deeds were done,
Komitas was still alive;
But his spirit had risen with those who were killed,
Without it, he could not survive.

Unable to work, a broken man -
His mind now tortured and wracked with grief -
Komitas languished in a sanitorium
Until God gave to him His Divine Relief.

ॐ

("Patarag" means "Divine Liturgy," in Armenian)

General Andranik Ozanian

Andranik was the most prominent figure in the Armenian struggle for national liberation in modern times.

Andranik

Like an eagle, he had soared;
Like a tiger, he had caught;
Like a fox, he had outwitted;
Like a lion, he had fought.

(continues on the next page)

Many an enemy, had he conquered;
Many a strike, had he planned;
Many a battle, had he won
For the sake of his people and land.

Committed to Armenia's liberation
From the young age of twenty-two,
He had never compromised his principles
For the selfishness of a few.

From Arakelotz to Zangezour,
His leadership had been supreme;
He was loved by all Armenians
who held him in highest esteem.

General Andranik Ozanian
Whose life was but a test
Of great resolve and sacrifice
Was finally laid to rest:

Like an eagle, he had soared;
Like a tiger, he had caught;
Like a fox, he had outwitted;
Like a lion, he had fought.

&

An Old Man

An Old man walks along a path
   Surrounded by a garden lush –
And suddenly, he comes to rest
   With ancient eyes that start to flush.

A vision of another walk
   Has escaped from the darkest cell
Of the prison deep within his mind
   From whence, for years, it had come to dwell.

(continues on the next page)

Familiar faces, sounds and places
Of a childhood not fulfilled –
Of a people – Peaceful – Loving
Doomed by Taalat to be killed.

And the walk that he relives
Through deserts full of death and pain –
Uprooted from an ancient homeland
By a nation truly gone insane.

Forced to walk, to thirst, to hunger –
Tortured, bludgeoned, maimed and murdered –
The tragic victims of great madness
Whose cries for mercy went unanswered.

A hopelessness so filled with terror –
A feeling that he cannot shake –
Reliving now, those days of horror –
The countless people that grim death did take.

He shakes his head – His body trembles –
Artesian wells, his eyes are now –
And looking up into the heavens
He asks his God "How could they" – "How?"

(continues on the next page)

How could Young Turks destroy a race –
    Such an asset to their way of life?
How dare they try to put an end
    To all Armenians by sword and knife?

He hears no answer coming forward –
    For madness has no logic great;
And he wonders was it Godsent -
    To test the strength of his people's faith?

Then, as he looks at all the flowers
    And the lushness, he now walks through
He knows that evil did not triumph –
    For all that perished, there lived a few.

Many years have since gone fleeting –
    And the remnants of his ancient race
Have been spread like seeds in strong wind
    To grow again – A new world to face.

And now the old man with new insight
    Knows that the walk of death and sorrow
Had meant the end of countless people
    But for Armenians a new tomorrow.

&

Images/Illustrations

Page	Title	Source	First Used
2	Wildflowers	Marjorie Rodgers	Love Poems FC&L
3	Chain w/ Heart	BSP/Oakozhan	LoveAndRomance360.com
4	Roman Vase	Roman 2ⁿᵈ Century	Poems on Love, L&H
5	Sailing Boats	Marjorie Rodgers	Love Poems FC&L
8	Couple / Love is Life	BSP/ KostiantynVoitenko	Poems on Love, L&H
11	Couple Dancing	BSP/MEGGJ	Poems on Love, L&H
12	Microscope	Home Science Tools	Poems on Love, L&H
13	Earth w/Moonrise	Google/NASA	Poems on Love, L&H
15	Man w/Smartphone	BSP/StudioRomantic	Poems on Love, L&H
17	I Love You in Sand	BSP/nruboc	Poems on Love, L&H
19	How Do I Love Thee	BSP/fat_fa_tin	Poems on Love, L&H
22	Couple in Garden	BSP/ Michael Shake	Electpress Channel
24	Two Swallows	BSP/Nataba	Poems on Love, L&H
28	Couple Visiting Venice	BSP/Kaspars Grinvalds	LoveAndRomance360.com
30	Portrait of Model	BSP/ photoCD	LoveAndRomance360.com
33	Couple in Love	BSP/ Oneinchpunch	LoveAndRomance360.com
34	Two Friends At a Bar	BSP/Wayhome Studio	Poems on Love, L&H
37	Pensive Man	BSP/89788500	LoveAndRomance360.com
38	Happy Couple on Beach	BSP/VH-studio	Poems on Love, L&H
39	Kissing Couple	BSP/ ruslan_shramko	LoveAndRomance360.com
40	Harbor of Love	Ara J. Movsesian	Poems on Love, L&H
41	Pearls in Shell	BSP/Volff	Poems on Love, L&H
43	Oriental Woman	BSP/kalim	LoveAndRomance360.com
47	NGC-4414	Google/NASA	Poems on Love, L&H
49	Melting Snow	West Central Tribune	Poems on Love, L&H
52	Iguazu Falls	Nat World Safaris	Poems on Love, L&H
54	Forest Animals	Marjorie Rodgers	Love Poems FC&L
56	Crocodile	Nat Geographic	Poems on Love, L&H
57	Hippopotamus	BSP/Arepiv	Poems on Love, L&H
60	Kangaroo with Joey	BSP/Lindsey_Images	Poems on Love, L&H
62	Two Happy Boys	BSP/Tuzenko	Poems on Love, L&H
65	Excited Boy Fishing	BSP/Everest Comm	Poems on Love, L&H
68	Holy Redeemer Church	Ara J. Movsesian	Armenia: A Journey TH
71	Mount Ararat	Ara J. Movsesian	Armenia: A Journey TH
73	Vardan/Avarayr	Keghouni 1903	Armenia: A Journey TH
75	David of Sasoun	Ara J. Movsesian	Armenia: A Journey TH
77	David of Sasoun	Ara J. Movsesian	Armenia: A Journey TH
78	Etchmiadzin	Ara J. Movsesian	Armenia: A Journey TH
81/82	Holy Cross/Aghtamar	Ara J. Movsesian	Armenia: A Journey TH
83/84	Walls of Ani / Ani Cathedral	Ara J. Movsesian	Armenia: A Journey TH
85	Komitas Vardapet	Image from Archives	Armenia: A Journey TH
87	Armenian Genocide	Image from Archives	Armenia: A Journey TH
88	Andranik Ozanian	Image from Archives	Armenia: A Journey TH
90	The Desert March	Reuters	Poems on Love, L&H

Other Titles by
Ara John Movsesian

Pearls of Love:
How to Write Love Letters & Love Poems
Publisher: The Electric Press®
Trade Paperback: 320 pages
ISBN-13: 978-0916919-40-5

Pearls of Love:
English – Spanish Bilingual Edition
Publisher: The Electric Press®
Trade Paperback: 566 pages
ISBN-13: 978-0916919-43-6

Love Poems for Cards & Letters
Publisher: The Electric Press®
Trade Paperback: 96 pages
ISBN-13: 978-0916919-04-7

Rinny Raccoon
Publisher: The Electric Press®
Trade Paperback: 36 pages
ISBN-13: 978-0916919-73-3

A History Book
Published by
The Electric Press®

ARMENIA: A Journey Through History

Written by: Arra S. Avakian, Sc.D.
Poetry By: Ara John Movsesian

Language: English
Trade Paperback: 352 pages
ISBN-13: 978-0916919-24-5
Item Weight: 1.04 pounds
Dimensions: 6 x 0.8 x 9 inches

About the Author

Ara John Movsesian was born on June 16, 1949, in Troy, New York. In 1955, he and his family moved to California's San Joaquin Valley and settled in the city of Fresno where he spent his childhood and adolescence.

While still in his teens, he began to write songs for personal enjoyment and a love of poetry grew out of this pastime. Perhaps the fact that his mother was an accomplished poet in her native language, Armenian, helped inspire him to begin this life-long endeavor.

In 1969, Ara entered the University of California at Berkeley from where, in 1974, he graduated with a Master's Degree in Architecture. He is a licensed architect and poet whose works have touched many lives.

To him, his vocation and avocation are interrelated endeavors. "One cannot separate Writing, a romantic and creative process, from Architecture, a visionary profession." They both require inspiration, technical ability and discipline. These Collected Poems are from his published and non-published works. In 2021, Ara retired from his corporate position to spend more time pursuing creative endeavors.

ॐ

Made in the USA
Columbia, SC
24 February 2023

12829119R00059